Anemone Fish

by Leighton Taylor

Lerner Publications Company • Minneapolis

This book is dedicated to all the kind people who helped me to learn to read and to write—two of life's great gifts.
                                                                —LT

This book uses the term anemone fish *for ease of reading. The scientific spelling is* anemonefish.

The photographs in this book are used with permission of: © Stephen Frink/CORBIS, pp. 4, 18, 23, 28; © age fotostock/SuperStock, pp. 6, 8, 9, 10, 12, 14, 15, 17, 20, 21, 22, 24, 25, 26, 27, 29, 30, 36, 37, 38, 40, 42, 43, 46; © Laura Westlund/Independent Picture Service, p. 5; © Andrew Dawson/SuperStock, p. 7; © Hal Beral /V&W/SeaPics.com, pp. 11, 32; © Prisma/ SuperStock, 13; © TARIK TINAZAY/AFP/Getty Images, p. 16; © Douglas P. Wilson; Frank Lane Picture Agency/CORBIS, p. 19; © Photononstop/SuperStock, p. 31; © Stuart Westmorland/ CORBIS, p. 33; © Lawson Wood/CORBIS, p. 34; © Espen Rekdal/SeaPics.com, p. 35; © STR/SFP/Getty Images, p. 39; © AFP/Getty Images, p. 41; © Tom Brakefield/SuperStock, p. 47; © STR/AFP/Getty Images, p. 48 (top); © Ernest Manewal/SuperStock, p. 48 (bottom).

Front Cover: © David B. Fleetham/SeaPics.com.

Lerner Publications Company
A division of Lerner Publishing Group
241 First Avenue North
Minneapolis, Minnesota 55401 U.S.A.

Website address: www.lernerbooks.com

Library of Congress Cataloging-in-Publication Data

Taylor, L. R. (Leighton R.)
    Anemone fish / by Leighton Taylor.
       p.   cm. — (Early bird nature books)
    Includes index.
    ISBN-13: 978–0–8225–6467–6 (lib. bdg. : alk. paper)
    ISBN-10: 0–8225–6467–X (lib. bdg. : alk. paper)
    1. Anemonefishes—Juvenile literature. I. Title. II. Series.
QL638.P77T39 2007
597'.72—dc22   2006006455

Manufactured in the United States of America
1 2 3 4 5 6 – JR – 12 11 10 09 08 07

Contents

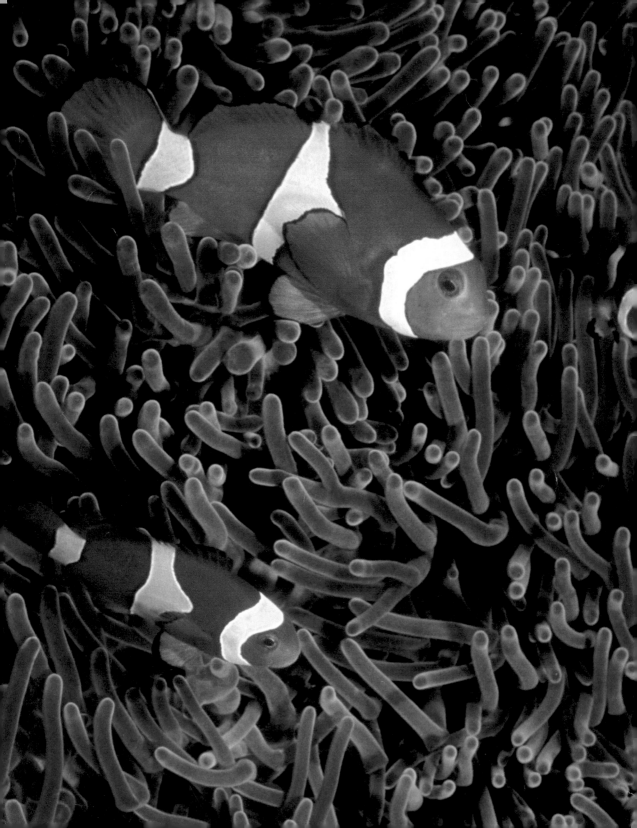

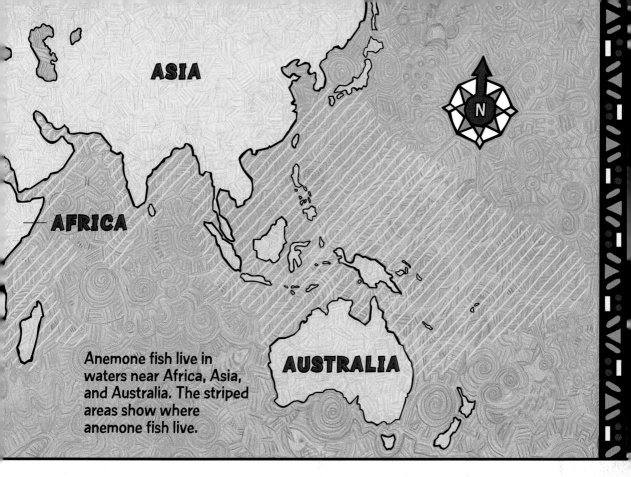

ASIA

AFRICA

AUSTRALIA

N

Anemone fish live in waters near Africa, Asia, and Australia. The striped areas show where anemone fish live.

Be a Word Detective

Can you find these words as you read about the anemone fish's life? Be a detective and try to figure out what they mean. You can turn to the glossary on page 46 for help.

anemone
clown fish
coral reef
corals
gills

habitat
hatch
mucus
pollution

symbiosis
tentacles
tropics
zooplankton

Chapter 1

These are anemone (uh-NEM-uh-nee) fish. Can you name the oceans where anemone fish live?

The Anemone Fish

 Anemone fish live in warm, tropical oceans. They are found in the Pacific Ocean, the Indian Ocean, and the Red Sea. They also live in warm waters near Australia.

The world has 28 kinds of anemone fish. Most of them are brightly colored. All of them are smaller than your hand. Some are even smaller than your thumb.

Anemone fish can be many different sizes. But none of the fish are very big.

A few kinds of anemone fish are also called clown fish. Maybe this is because their bodies are orange and white. Such bright colors remind people of clowns.

Do you think clown fish is a good name for these animals?

Anemone fish have two fins on their sides. These are called pectoral (PEHK-tor-uhl) fins. They also have a fin on their back. This is called a dorsal (DOHR-suhl) fin. Fins help the anemone fish swim.

Anemone fish use their fins to swim. They also use their fins to move water. Moving water cleans dirt away from the fish's home.

This is a spine cheek anemone fish. Like all fish, it uses gills to breathe.

Anemone fish can breathe underwater. They use gills to get air from water. Water goes into the mouth of an anemone fish. Then the water passes over the gills. Finally, the water comes out through slits on the fish's sides. You can't see the gills of an anemone fish. They are under a special cover. But you can see the slits where water comes out.

Anemone fish have big eyes. They also have big mouths. They can see tiny animals floating in the water. Anemone fish gulp the animals into their mouths.

Anemone fish use their large eyes to look for food floating in the ocean.

Chapter 2

This is a coral reef. Anemone fish live on coral reefs. Where do coral reefs grow?

Home and Food

The type of place where a kind of animal lives is called a habitat (HAB-uh-tat). The habitat of anemone fish is the coral reef. Many kinds of animals and plants live on coral reefs.

Coral reefs are found in clear ocean waters. The reefs need a lot of sun. The sun helps warm the water where the reefs grow.

Reefs grow in a special part of the world. This part of the world is called the tropics. The tropics are near the equator. The equator is an imaginary band that goes around Earth like a belt.

Scuba divers sometimes explore coral reefs.

Coral reefs are made mainly by animals. The animals are called corals. Many coral animals live together in a big group. Each coral animal grows a hard, stony skeleton around and under itself. A coral's stony skeleton joins those of its neighbors. These skeletons help to make coral reefs.

Special plants grow on coral reefs. These plants can also make skeletons. Plant skeletons help form coral reefs too.

These are corals. A coral's skeleton is very different from a human's skeleton. A coral's skeleton grows on the outside of the coral.

Anemone fish live with another animal on coral reefs. This animal is called the anemone. Anemones are related to corals. But they do not have skeletons. Anemone fish take their name from anemones.

Anemone fish were named for anemones. Can you find the fish that lives with this anemone?

An anemone fish cannot live without its anemone. The anemone is the fish's home. The fish finds food near its anemone. It raises its family near the anemone. Anemone fish spend most of their time in, under, and over their anemones.

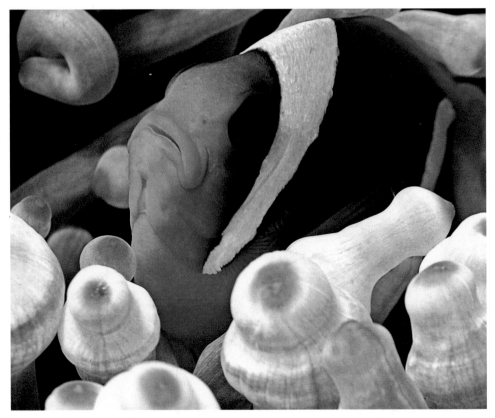

This anemone fish rests in its anemone.

An anemone makes a good hiding place for an anemone fish.

Anemones have tentacles (TEN-tuh-kuhlz). Tentacles are long and flexible. Anemones use them to feed, feel, and to protect themselves. Anemone fish sometimes hide in their anemone's tentacles.

Nearly one thousand kinds of anemones live in the oceans of the world. Some live deep underwater. Some live in icy seas. But only 10 kinds are home to anemone fish. These are often called carpet anemones. Their long tentacles can look like a shag carpet. And they are about the size of a small rug. That is how they got their name.

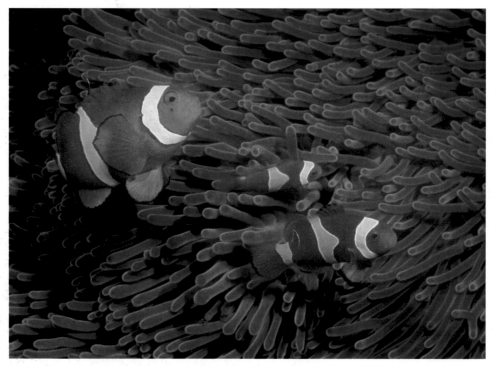

A carpet anemone looks a little like a shag carpet.

Most kinds of anemone fish eat tiny animals that float past the anemone. These tiny floating animals are called zooplankton (zoo-PLANGK-tuhn). Water moving over the anemone brings this floating food close to home.

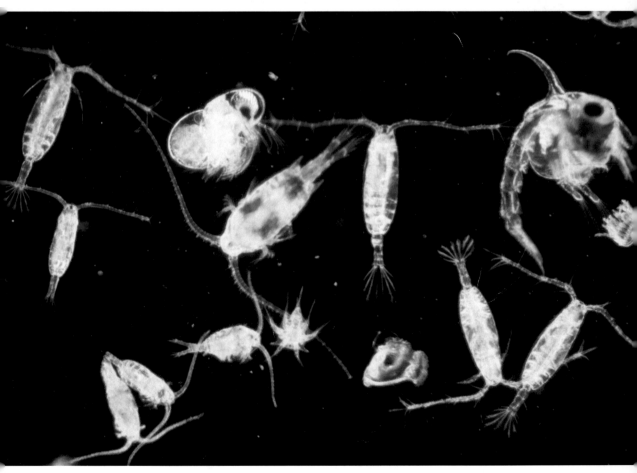

Anemone fish eat tiny floating animals like these.

Some kinds of anemone fish eat plants.
The plants grow on rocky places on the reef.
Sometimes the fish eat all the plants near
their anemone.

Plants grow on coral reefs.

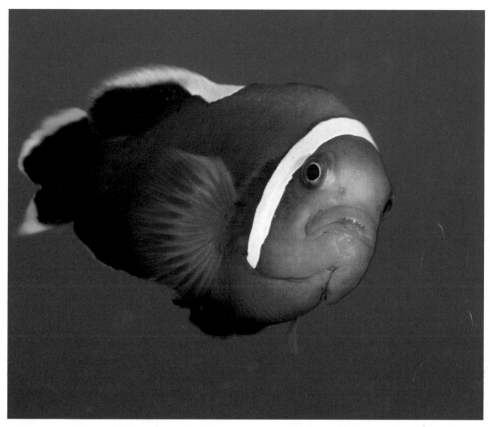

A large anemone fish may swim far from its anemone to find food.

Sometimes not much food is near the anemone. There may be only enough food for smaller anemone fish. Then larger fish may leave to find food. They might travel far away for a few hours. While they are gone, the smaller fish stay close to the anemone.

Chapter 3

These pink anemone fish stay safe in their anemone. But anemones don't make good homes for most fish. Do you know why?

Special Protection

 Anemone fish are some of the only fish that can live with anemones. That is because anemones are poisonous.

An anemone's tentacles are covered with tiny sacs. Each sac holds a dart. The darts are soaked in poison. When something touches the sac, it bursts open. The poison dart flies out. The dart is so tiny that you can see it only with a microscope (MY-cro-scope). This tool makes small things look big.

An anemone's tentacles can shoot poison darts.

An anemone's poison darts have sharp points. The darts can stick to anything that touches the anemone's tentacles. Darts can hurt. Sometimes they kill. But anemones don't usually fire darts at their own anemone fish.

Anemone tentacles do not harm this fish.

Why don't anemones fire darts at anemone fish? Anemone fish make mucus (MYOO-kuhss) in their skin. Mucus is slimy. All fish are covered with mucus. But an anemone fish's mucus is special. It tells the anemone that the fish won't harm it.

The mucus on the bodies of these fish helps to protect them.

If an anemone fish is taken away from anemones, it loses its special mucus. When the fish is returned to its anemone home, the anemone will shoot darts at the fish. The anemone does not recognize its old guest.

Anemone fish are safe from anemone darts only if they live near anemones.

Touching an anemone's tentacles restores an anemone fish's mucus.

When an anemone fish has been away from its anemone, the fish must regain its special mucus. It quickly and gently touches the anemone over and over. After several days, it regains its special covering. Then the anemone will no longer shoot darts at the fish.

This is a butterfly fish. Butterfly fish sometimes nibble on anemones.

Anemones protect anemone fish from other fish. Anemone fish swim into their anemone when other fish come near.

Anemone fish protect anemones too. The anemone's poison darts don't hurt a fish called the butterfly fish. Some butterfly fish try to eat the anemone's tentacles. But anemone fish chase away the butterfly fish.

Living together helps both the anemone fish and the anemones. Scientists have a name for this shared life. They call it symbiosis (sihm-be-OH-sihs). This word comes from two Greek words meaning "living together." Plants and animals that live together in this way have a better chance of staying alive than if they lived alone.

The relationship between anemones and anemone fish is an example of symbiosis.

Chapter 4

Anemone fish live in groups. Which fish is the biggest in the group?

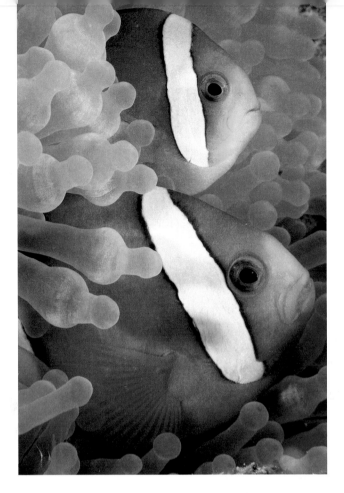

Raising Young

Anemone fish live in small groups. Usually only one family lives in one anemone. The fish in the group are different sizes. The biggest fish is the mother.

The other fish are all males. The second biggest fish is the father. He will help the mother when she lays her eggs.

Female anemone fish lay eggs. Then male fish help to take care of the eggs.

The mother lays eggs when she is ready to have babies. Babies will hatch from the eggs. The mother chooses a clean spot on a rock. She lays her eggs under an edge of the anemone's floppy body.

These are the eggs of a clown fish.

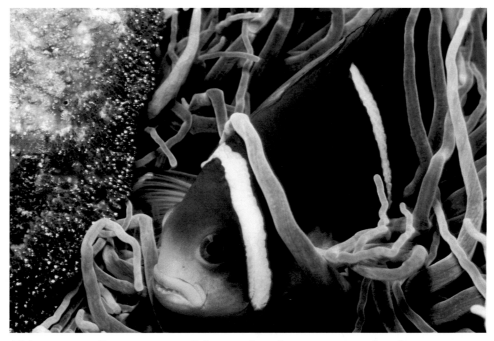

This orange fin anemone fish watches its eggs very closely.

The mother fish sticks her eggs to the rock. Then the father goes to work. He must keep the eggs clean. He makes sure the water on the eggs is fresh. He fans and paddles his fins to push clear water over the eggs. He also removes sand from the eggs. He uses his mouth to pick up the sand.

The father guards the eggs too. He chases away other fish. They may try to eat the eggs.

Baby anemone fish hatch at night.

After about one week, one tiny fish hatches out of each egg. The baby fish look very different from their parents. They have clear bodies and big, dark eyes. A baby anemone fish is about the size of a child's fingernail clipping.

A baby anemone fish does not live with its parents. It floats away after it hatches. It drifts around for about three weeks.

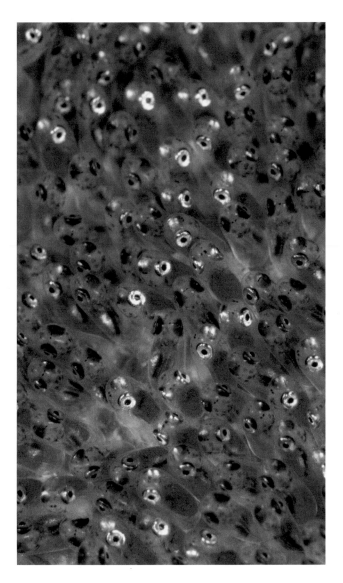

These are baby anemone fish.

Finally, the young anemone fish finds its own anemone. It stops floating. It swims down to its new home. It settles into its anemone. The young fish becomes the same color as its parents. Someday it may lay or guard eggs of its own.

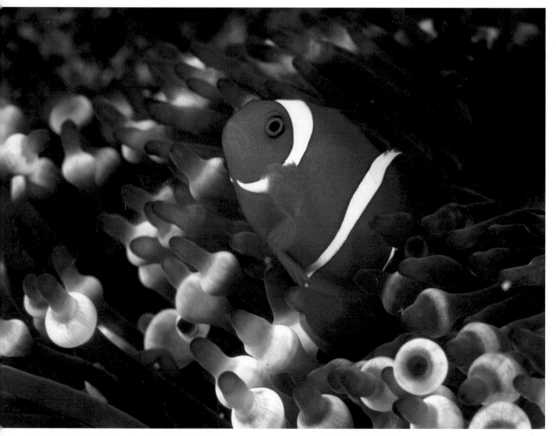

This brightly colored fish has reached adulthood.

Chapter 5

Anemone fish are beautiful, but they face dangers. What is one danger anemone fish face?

Dangers for Anemone Fish

Many people like anemone fish. The fish are fun to watch. They are often bright and colorful. But wild anemone fish face many dangers. One danger is not having a place to live.

Coral reefs are home to a variety of plant and animal life.

Anemone fish need coral reefs to live on. Coral reefs are very important to the world. They are homes to millions of plants and animals. Many reefs around the world are in danger.

Storms and big waves can break reefs apart. But these are natural dangers. Reefs can survive them. Humans bring new dangers.

These reefs are part of the Great Barrier Reef. The great Barrier Reef is near Australia.

Scientists are very concerned about the dangers coral reefs face.

Putting up buildings near the ocean can hurt coral reefs. Bulldozers push away dirt to make room for buildings. Rainwater washes the dirt into the sea. The dirt makes the water cloudy and muddy. Coral reefs need clear water to live.

Pollution (puh-LOO-shuhn) can hurt reefs too. Pollution makes the land, air, and water dirty. Spilled oil and discarded plastic cups and bags are pollution. They hurt and kill all ocean life.

Pollution has hurt the Great Barrier Reef. This worker is inspecting corals on the reef.

If the ocean water becomes too warm, reefs may be in danger.

Coral reefs need warm water to live. But water that is too warm kills corals. Scientists have learned that the ocean is getting warmer every year. Reefs are beginning to die in many areas.

When reefs are destroyed, anemone fish have nowhere to live. Thousands of other kinds of animals and plants also have nowhere to live. We need to take good care of the world's coral reefs.

By taking care of coral reefs, we can help make sure anemone fish stay around for years to come.

A NOTE TO ADULTS
ON SHARING A BOOK

When you share a book with a child, you show that reading is important. To get the most out of the experience, read in a comfortable, quiet place. Turn off the television and limit other distractions, such as telephone calls.

Be prepared to start slowly. Take turns reading parts of this book. Stop occasionally and discuss what you're reading. Talk about the photographs. If the child begins to lose interest, stop reading. When you pick up the book again, revisit the parts you have already read.

BE A VOCABULARY DETECTIVE

The word list on page 5 contains words that are important in understanding the topic of this book. Be word detectives and search for the words as you read the book together. Talk about what the words mean and how they are used in the sentence. Do any of these words have more than one meaning? You will find the words defined in a glossary on page 46.

WHAT ABOUT QUESTIONS?

Use questions to make sure the child understands the information in this book. Here are some suggestions:

What did this paragraph tell us? What does this picture show? What do you think we'll learn about next? Where do anemone fish live? Could an anemone fish live near your home? Why/why not? What is a coral reef? What is an anemone? What do you think it's like being an anemone fish? What is your favorite part of this book? Why?

If the child has questions, don't hesitate to respond with questions of your own, such as What do *you* think? Why? What is it that you don't know? If the child can't remember certain facts, turn to the index.

INTRODUCING THE INDEX

The index helps readers find information without searching through the whole book. Turn to the index on page 48. Choose an entry such as *food* and ask the child to use the index to find out what anemone fish eat. Repeat this exercise with as many entries as you like. Ask the child to point out the differences between an index and a glossary. (The index helps readers find information, while the glossary tells readers what words mean.)

LEARN MORE ABOUT
ANEMONE FISH

BOOKS

Earle, Sylvia A. *Hello, Fish! Visiting the Coral Reef.* Washington, DC: National Geographic Society, 1999. Bright pictures and interesting text introduce twelve different kinds of fish.

Johnson, Rebecca L. *A Journey into the Ocean.* Minneapolis: Carolrhoda Books, Inc., 2004. Take a tour of ocean plants and animals in this colorful book.

Pratt, Kristin Joy. *A Swim through the Sea*. Nevada City, CA: Dawn Publications, 1994. Learn more about ocean life in this fun alphabet book.

Simon, Seymour. *Oceans*. New York: Morrow Junior Books, 1990. In this book, you can read all about oceans.

WEBSITES

Clown Fish
   http://www.enchantedlearning.com/subjects/fish/printouts/ Clownfishprintout.shtml
   Visit this page to learn more about the clown fish.

Colorful Coral Reefs
   http://www.mbayaq.org/efc/efc_se/sz_colorful_coral.asp
   This website from California's Monterey Bay Aquarium includes detailed information about coral reefs.

Sea Anemone
   http://www.mnzoo.com/animals/discovery_bay/anemone.asp
   This site from the Minnesota Zoo features facts about sea anemones.

GLOSSARY

anemone (uh-NEM-uh-nee): a kind of ocean animal. Anemone fish live with anemones.

clown fish: a kind of anemone fish

coral reef: a large ridge made by plants and animals in warm, shallow seas. Millions of animals and plants live together on coral reefs.

corals: a kind of ocean animal related to the jelly fish. Corals help to make coral reefs.

gills: a part of the body that fish use to breathe. You cannot see an anemone fish's gills.

habitat (HAB-uh-tat): the type of place where a kind of animal lives

hatch: to break out of an egg

mucus (MYOO-kuhss): a slimy substance made by an animal. An anemone fish is covered with mucus.

pollution (puh-LOO-shuhn): things that make the land, air, and water dirty

symbiosis (sihm-be-OH-sihs): the name for the relationship between anemone fish and anemones. Symbiosis means living together.

tentacles (TEN-tuh-kuhlz): long, boneless limbs. Anemones have tentacles.

tropics: a warm, sunny part of the world. The tropics are near the equator.

zooplankton (zoo-PLANGK-tuhn): tiny animals that float in the sea. Most kinds of anemone fish eat zooplankton.

INDEX

Pages listed in **bold** type refer to photographs.